The Good Death and the Civil War:

The Haunting of an American Battlefield

John G. Sabol

C.A.S.P.E.R. Research Center

Also by John Sabol

Ghost Excavator (2007)

Ghost Culture (2007)

Gettysburg Unearthed (2007)

Battlefield Hauntscape (2008)

The Anthracite Coal Region (2008)

The Politics of Presence (2008)

Bodies of Substance, Fragments of Memory (2009)

Phantom Gettysburg (2009)

Digging Deep (2009)

The Re-Haunting(s) of Gettysburg (2010)

The Haunted Theatre (2011)

Ghost Culture Too (2012)

Beyond the Paranormal (2012)

Digging-Up Ghosts (2nd publishing, 2013)

Burnside Bridge (2013)

The Gettysburg Experience (2013)

The Absence Above, A Presence Below (2013)

The Production of Haunted Space (2013)

Centralia, Pennsylvania (2013)

The Ghost Excavation (2013)

The Good Death and the Civil War:

The Haunting of an American Battlefield

Ghost Excavator Books, Inc ™©

Bedford, Pennsylvania, USA

ISBN-13: 978-1494744434

ISBN-10: 1494744430

Ghost Excavation Books, Inc. ™©
A division of C.A.S.P.E.R. Research Center™©,
Bedford, PA, USA
www.ghostexcavation.com

"A lady once asked me if I believed in ghosts and apparitions. I answered, with truth and simplicity, 'No Madam! I have seen far too many myself!'".

- Samuel Taylor Coleridge

"Belief is the uncritical acceptance of something you can't prove."

- Hans Holzer

<u>The "Ghost World"</u>

The world of "ghosts" has changed. Once the haunt of "ghost hunters", for the past 125 years (or so), it has metamorphosed into "something" different. A "ghost" and its "haunted" nature has manifested into an influential conceptual metaphor (cf. Blanco and Peeren 2013) that has "appeared" in both popular (global) culture and academic circles. This involves **"exploring and illuminating phenomena other than the putative return of the dead" (Ibid: 2).**

A conceptual metaphor is a particular way of producing knowledge (Bal 2010:10). This knowledge production is <u>not</u> a "hunt" for the presence of the dead at haunted locations. Rather, it concerns a series of questions that can transmit knowledge across various social science disciplines (Blanco and Peeren 2013:2).

Two of these questions are important for my current research, as envisioned in this book. These are:

- **"the temporal and spatial sedimentation of history and tradition";** and
- **"the intricacies of memory and trauma" (Ibid: 2).**

This "spectral turn" of events will be re-turned back, in this book, to "ghosts" as the return of the dead, rather than its current broader use as a conceptual metaphor. History and tradition (as cultural belief and ritual practice) in particular times and places (spaces) remain important in this re-turn. Memory and the trauma of particular "end times" in specific spaces take "center stage" in this analysis, with a focus on the "theater of war".

When and how do past entities labeled "ghosts" become real within a particular social community? How do their manifestations "speak" of past agency, rather than present politics or the contemporary use of metaphor? These are not simple questions.

To seek answers, we must, like archaeologists, "excavate" backwards from a manifestation of presence to particular "agents" of that presence. In the specific case of an apparition, this agency may be the afterlife consciousness of an individual that remains after the physical death and decay of the body.

In this "excavation", we must depart from the notion that "ghosts" are inferred from their effects upon the environment (increases/decreases in ambient conditions; a manifestation of the presence of something "other" than what they were in life: "orbs", shadows, light anomalies, etc.). It is more constructive to begin with the hypothesis that, under certain conditions (and possibly until certain conditions are met) past interactive presence can (and do) manifest. This (these) condition(s), I propose, are cultural (not physical) in nature.

This book is an exploration of a particular kind of "ghost" or "specter", one that has its origin in pre-Civil War America, and one that evolved into a full-blown manifestation on contemporary Civil War battlefields. The context of this haunting becomes a critical element in understanding these "ghosts" and why they haunt. As Blanco and Peeren (2013) state:

"Historical events or memories....may give rise to vastly different hauntings....All history and memory may indeed be spectral in some sense, but understanding the effects of particular instances requires contextualization and conceptual delimitation" (2013:15).

Although Blanco and Peeren (2013) state that **"the post-1990 use of the ghost as no longer primarily a literal phenomenon requiring empirical verification" (2013:21),** in our research, the empirical verification of interactive past presence remains a critical part of the fieldwork.

Like the work of the conceptual metaphor, a "ghost excavation <u>also</u> focuses on "unearthing" those hidden **"and neglected aspects of the social and cultural realm, past and present"** **(Ibid: 21).** In both realms, it is a "turn" away from contemporary "ghost hunting", and its ignorance (in most cases) of the <u>past</u> social and cultural environments; and its (almost) total dependence on technology in the <u>present</u> to document and analyze those <u>potential</u> past occurrences of presence at haunted locations.

There is more to a haunting than deadly outcomes, and a "ghost" is more than an ephemeral metaphor. The power of culture, and its belief and ritual systems, play an important part. And I am not referring to the contemporary world.

In our fieldwork, the presence of apparitions is a <u>natural</u> occurrence. The apparition is viewed as an ethnographic informant, as we (during fieldwork) participate in <u>their</u> culture, and sense their behaviors and practices.

Bubandt (2012), among others, has treated "spirits" (or "ghosts") as informants during ethnographic fieldwork. During our fieldwork, in exploring the social realities of the production of haunted space, we facilitate the mediation and communication with "who" remains after particular events of a socially-produced space have ended. This we do through particular performance practices during the "excavation" process.

The Civil War battlefield "ghost" is no "family" ghost, though "home" and the family are important factors in their manifestations. These battlefield ghosts are not evoked (and certainly not provoked) in any ordinary way ("is anyone here?"; "show us a sign....make the lights blink...").

These "ghosts" require a surrogate: a specific, identifiable individual, such as a fellow soldier, a commanding officer, a family member. These are the roles that we enact in a "ghost excavation" on these battlefields.

It has been suggested that there are various **"regimes of communication" (Delaplace 2013)** between "ghosts" and people. Different societies have different patterns of interaction and communication. A "ghost excavation" is context-specific. We use different means of communication with the "ghost", itself dependent upon the cultural horizon we are "excavating".

Welcome, readers, to the "ghost world" of mid-19th c. America, and its "culture of war" and the "culture of death" that formed the social world and experiences of the Civil War soldier! What follows is the basis for "how" and "why" we do a particular form of fieldwork (the "ghost excavation") on these American Civil War battlefields.

Preface

This is a book about haunted battlefields where, in the majority of engagements, it was men who fought and died. The investigation of these haunted battlefields, however, is also a focus on women, and the importance of home and family. Both revolve around the experience of death, preparation for that death, and its relation to the end of life as a "good death".

This is a different perception of war, battle, and the battlefield. It is not about who won and who lost. With death, nobody wins. And suffering does not end as an official notification about a family member who has died in war.

In *Landscapes of the Western Front: Materiality During the Great War* (2012), Ross J. Wilson has said this about the study of "war cultures". This involves:

"The multiple meanings and perceptions that individuals and groups, at home and on the front lines, created in response to the conflict to endure its effects" (2012:9).

One particular "culture of war", that of the American Civil War, was framed by particular belief systems and ritual acts (the "culture of death"). The result of mixing these "cultures" on the battlefield led, I propose, to "haunted" Civil War battlefields.

The concepts of the "good death" and "domestic imagery" (the importance of "home" and family), as part of this "culture of death", led, in some instances, to the reason "why" a Civil War soldier would continue to remain on the battlefield, even after 150 years.

Many of these "ghost soldiers", enculturated in the "culture of death", and regardless of religious affiliation or background, still "wait" for the proper rituals associated with dying at "home". These soldiers, as an active consciousness of personal biographies, remain because they are still not "home".

There were many kinds of death in the American Civil War that went beyond the battlefield. These other deaths are, in the majority, not a minority. These included death by disease, starvation, guerilla warfare, food shortages, accidents, civilian casualties, and military confinement, to name a few.

My focus here, however, is on battlefield death, the "bad" death, quick and with unattended consequences: its possibility, its spatiality, and its actuality as a particular way of ending a life.

What was the impact of this death, after the armies moved on, and the battlefield appeared "clean" of remains and the debris of combat? Did something, perhaps someone (or someone's memory of it all) still remain? If so, why? Was something unfulfilled, not accomplished, some words that remained to be spoken or written as that final gesture or message?

This is a book about understanding how these soldiers wanted to die, and what happened when that did not occur. That it did, and often on these battlefields, may well attest to what occurred when a ritual, part of an important belief system, was not finalized.

What happens when (for example) a week after the battle of Antietam (September 17, 1862), a Union medical officer reported the following: **"The dead were almost wholly unburied...."** Where is the "good death" in this? A call of "victory" is a shallow phrase here.

Desperate acts like **"throwing them** (the dead) **into pits like dead chickens"** replaced the "home" and family plot, and the ritual that was called (and involved) the "good death". The consequences this may have had will be outlined here, manifesting (in time) as the birth of Civil War battlefield hauntings.

These de-humanizing events that occurred in the early battles was replaced, still inadequately, in later engagements during the war. Fellow soldiers tried to complete these rituals of the "good death". A "band of brothers" (those related to one another, and those who enlisted and fought together) became real "bands of brothers" to dying men, serving as surrogates for the loved ones at home:

- They recorded the burial places;
- They wrote notes and interred them with the dead;
- They listened to the dying man's final words; and if they survived

- They conveyed these dying thoughts to the dead soldier's family at home.

The "home front", and its domestic imagery (family, and especially "Mother") became a "battlefield home front".

Still, about half of the dead were never identified, remaining "lost", missing in action. How many of these soldiers were never accorded any of the proper rituals of the "good death"? That number, once known, will tell us "who" and how many haunt these battlefields.

The American Civil War changed the course of social history of mid-19th c. American society. It altered the image of the afterlife, a "ghost", and the role of women outside the household. It was not so much the trauma of the horrors of war (that "culture of war"), or not knowing one is "dead", that produced these "ghosts".

It was the dying far from "home" and family without the proper rituals of the "culture of death" being observed and enacted that produced the haunting. This is their story, a "ghost story" of those who remain, waiting to go "home"...

Photo 1: Who Remains from this Battle Today?

Table of Contents

<u>*Photographs/Illustrations*</u>

Introduction

Archaeologist Jacquetta Hawkes, in her **"Guide to the Prehistoric and Roman Monuments of England and Wales" (1951)** has said:

".....perhaps places where men had felt intensely and acted violently never quite rid themselves of the effects; perhaps, such feelings are created only in the minds of later beholders – yet even so, their survival is real".

One such place where men **"felt intensely and acted violently"** was an American Civil War battlefield. But not <u>all</u> battlefields are haunted; not even <u>all</u> American Civil War battlefields.

During the American Civil War, a "lived" experience occurred in mass in particular physical environments (camps and battlefields) which most soldiers, as "civilians", never experienced before (especially a Southern soldier). One such place, the battlefield, became a large-scale environmental ensemble or "place ballet".

These locations, as interactions of individual and group bodily routines ("drills"), rooted in particular spaces (the K.O.C.O.A.) became, because of massive deadly outcomes, an important site of place attachment for both the living and the dead. This concept of place attachment had the potential of transforming these battlefield spaces into a (continuing) lived space with a unique character and ambiance.

The Civil War battlefield changed, I propose, from an initial visual "landscape" (pre-battle) to a auditory (heard) "soundscape" (during battle):

> **"Hasten Brothers, to the battle,**
>
> **Loud the bugle sounds afar;**
>
> **I am weary, wounded, dying,**
>
> **But I hear the call for war".**

- *Hasten Brothers to the Battle* (words by Theodore D.C. Miller).

The experience of battle assaulted a soldier's sensorium. The drills did not prepare them for what they were to experience on these battlefields.

Sight was at a premium. It was surprising for them how little they could actually see. During the first major battle, Bull Run (or Manassas Junction):

"when the Rhode Islanders lay down – and they often did – they found that all they could make out was the red Virginia soil beneath them....But mostly their foe was invisible....factor reducing visibility was the smoke billowing from all the muskets and cannon....no breezes wafted the smoke away from the battlefield, so it hung like a London fog between the two sides...." (Detzer 2004:256-57).

This obscurity of perception became a commonality of experience for the Civil War soldier on the battlefield, as was the ensuing sounds of war:

"the gasping, the panting, the grunting of men....the ripping open of cartridges, the rattle of ramrods plunging into musket barrels, the clink of canteens against metal, the squealing wheels of artillery vehicles, the drum signals, the shouting and swearing" (Ibid: 257).

This was the sight(lessness) and sound of the "culture of war" on a Civil War battlefield. Does this experience of the battlefield remain today at these locations? Today, many of these Civil War battlefields are considered "ghostscapes" (for many paranormal investigators). These "haunted" ("ghostscape") battlefields are unique sensoriums, but not, I propose, places of "paranormal" events.

As Relph (1981) said: "We must attend **'carefully to the particularity of places and situations. It is the attempt to see clearly what there is' " (1981:177).** This is not "alienating" these battlefields, marking them exclusive, calling them "paranormal" sites. It is "excavating" what remains!

Still, why are some perceived to be haunted, and others not? Rudyard Kipling, the author of many fine novels, kept **"six honest serving men"** who taught him all his knowledge. Their names were: "How?", "Where?", "When?", "Why?", "What?", and "Who?" <u>These</u> are the six "ghosts" of the battlefield. It is these "ghosts", I propose, who will determine which American Civil War battlefields are really haunted.....

Regarding a battlefield haunting, there is less concern with what actually happened in the past than in exploring what remains of that event as a mode of present experience:

"If the historical past be knowable, it must belong to the present world of experience; if it be unknowable, history is worse than futile, it is impossible" (Oakeshott 1933:107).

In our investigations of haunted American Civil War battlefields, in fieldwork I label a "ghost excavation" (Cf. Sabol 2013), we are not focused on "re-enacting" what has been recorded as history, as much as how and why these soldiers fought and what happened when they died on the battlefield. This is an experiential (ethnographic) approach, a radical participation of "what happened there". Our investigations are not a detached measurement of ambient space.

An important research question is how to reduce a seemingly multi-layered world of mid-19th c. society into a finite one of social norms and perceptions that were involved in a particular production of past space (the Civil War battlefield):

"There is no perception which is not full of memories....what you have to explain....is not how perception arises, but how it is limited...." (Bergson (1908) 1988:33).

This is a focus on how <u>their</u> perceptions on the battlefield were physically limiting: an emphasis on the auditory, rather than the visual (due to intense smoke from gun and cannon fire). What remains of this battlefield event should form part of this limiting perception, and <u>our</u> experience of it today.

On a Civil War battlefield, these limiting perceptions were <u>also</u> cultural in nature. This involves the "habits" (learned through drills) of the "culture of war", and the "beliefs" (learned at home) of the "culture of death".

Without some sense of how a Civil War battlefield, and dying on a Civil War battlefield, was "culturally-attuned", there is no accurate (or authentic) means of determining "what" remains and "who" continues to manifest today. We need context, not measurement. This requires a participatory aesthetics rather than a detached observer attuned to electronic devices or a TV monitor.

To become a "witness" to what happened there then, and "who" may remain there today, one must understand the historical facts (the "culture of war") and the culture that wrote those facts (the "culture of death"). One must comprehend how important research into these historical facts and culture are, and how they intersect with a contemporary experience on these battlefields today.

Photo 2: The American Civil War Battlefield

The Battle of Bethel, 1861

<u>*The Archaeological Record*</u>

"No space ever vanishes utterly leaving no trace".

- Henri Lefebvre, <u>The Production of Space</u>

<u>Photo 3: What Remains of this Battlefield Space?</u>

The Battle of Shiloh, 1862

Photo 4: What Remains of this Battlefield Space?

Occupying Federal Troops

The perception of a contemporary battlefield presence is not an "entertaining" thought:

"The more we experience what the war was like, the more uncomfortable we should become….and we should be uncomfortable whenever we catch a glimpse of it".

- **(Gramm 2002: XIV).**

Henry Glassie (1977) in **"Archaeology and Folklore: Common Anxieties, Common Hopes in Historical Archaeology and the Importance of Material Things"** has said:

"The past is too important to leave to historians. The human reality is too important to leave to novelists".

I say the continuing human presence of past productions of battlefield space is too important to leave to most "ghost hunts". What we need is a social science-based fieldwork at these haunted locations. For me, haunted locations are fragmented representations of past productions of human cultural space. As an archaeologist, I begin with this: This happened here! What or "Who" remains? But what does this involve? First,

"Science in the most general sense is an attempt to learn as much as possible about the world in as many ways as possible with the sole restriction that what is claimed as knowledge be both testable and attainable by everyone" (Watson 1991:276).

This approach to science effectively eliminates the claims of mystics, psychics, and intuitionists, among others. Their "evidence" is based on "special" experiences, capabilities, or faith that is <u>not</u> in the domain of <u>public</u> experience. By public, I mean ordinary, not "paranormal" experiences. The important question in fieldwork becomes: how do we document what's left? I begin (not end) with the following:

"To establish one's explanations, one must predict things about the archaeological record based on already accepted facts....and then find that these predictions are themselves fulfilled on examination of the record" (Watson 1991:276).

Most of the time, these remains are invisible and undocumented, until the "excavation" begins. This fieldwork, therefore, involves (to a large extent) the use of the **"archaeological imagination"**, defined by Stanford archaeologist Michael Shanks as:

"a pervasive set of attitudes towards traces and remains, toward memory, time, and temporality" (2012:25).

We agree with Robin Wooffitt's call for a **"sociological parapsychology" (2010)**, as a location and culture-specific approach:

"But anomalous experiences, whatever their nature, are inextricably implicated in precisely the social processes and contexts which cannot be reproduced in laboratory conditions" (2010:73).

We cannot substitute the lab for actually being there on the battlefield; nor can a controlled and sanitized laboratory environment substitute for the movements through a horrific battlefield space, as a form of ritual or cultural performance (cf. John Carman 1999). These "ritualistic" acts on the battlefield, such as "drills", the use of sound cues as "sound marks" (particular drum rolls and bugle calls), and the wearing of "colors", created a particular sense of experience and semiotic meaning. What is left of these particular memories cannot be reproduced in the lab, but it can, I propose, be "unearthed" in the field on these battlefields.

An "excavation" of these remains is limited to what remains in the archaeological record of a particular landscape, nothing more. That this past presence is incomplete is <u>normal</u>, not "paranormal". An "excavation" deals with the past productions of space and what remains of those productions, both physical and sensory. We work with those remains. This is a re-constitution of the past, and not the re-enactment of past events. The work is ethnographic, but the focus is on <u>past</u>, not present, cultural behavior and belief.

In a recent article in North American Archaeology, the authors stress the **"special nature of Civil War sites" (Espenshade, Jolley, and Blegg 2002:41).** Part of this "special nature" is the fact that the **"battlefield dead were not comprehensively removed from the battlefield" (Ibid: 41).** Today, it is difficult to identify where these grave sites are located because

"unlike typical cemeteries, there is often a lack of formal, carefully aligned, grave features" (Ibid: 43).

Thus, many Civil War soldiers are still "missing in action (MIA). This has significance to "what", and perhaps "who" still "haunts these battlefields.

The authors also stress the importance of archaeologists using Inherent Military Probability (or I.M.P.) in their analysis of these sites:

"learn and apply the concept of IMP....requires the archaeologist to think like a Civil War soldier" (Ibid: 60).

In another book, Orr (1994) has said this:

"Battlefield sites....always, they must be linked to the anthropological values of the battle's participants...." (1994:33).

This is what we do in a "ghost excavation". Without some sense of how a Civil War battlefield was produced, and how the experience of death there is "culturally-attuned", there is no way to determine what remains <u>and</u> "who" continues as an active presence there. We need socio-cultural context for this, not a measurement of the contemporary ambient environment. This requires a participatory aesthetics rather than a detached observer who is attuned to electronic devices or a TV monitor, waiting for something to occur.

The "excavation" and perception of what remains is a reduction of what occurred in the past. This has important consequences:

"There is no perception which is not full of memories....what you have to explain....is not how perception arises, but how it is limited...." (Bergson (1908) 1988:40).

On a haunted American Civil War battlefield, one must not anticipate what may manifest; you must explain why manifestations are limited to space-specific elements of productions that occurred in the past, and that these manifesting elements are traces, vestiges, and fragments of performances that occurred there in the past.

These remains include residual sensory expressions or recordings and, in some cases, a consciousness of a particular human socio-cultural intelligence, who at times exhibits a variety of expressive phenomenon (cf. Maher and Hanson 1995). This consciousness is a memory of some aspects of former personhood that continues after the death of the physical body. This personhood may be the:

"existence of occurrent mental states belonging to a deceased individual....also the persistence of dispositional states (memories, traits, attitudes, abilities, etc.)" (Braude 2003: 294).

The manifestations that occur on haunted battlefields could be a form of social and/or mental field (cf. Sheldrake 2012), and one based on **"experiences had by the person with whose physical body was formerly associated as a kind of field"** **(Broad 1962:430).** This field is perceived as a **"series of mental states connected by continuity of character and memory"** **(Quinton 1975:65).**

Photo 5: Is This a Manifesting Social Field of Former Past Presence?

Antietam, Confederate in a ditch

Photo 6: Is This a Social Field of Former Past Presence?

Civil War – Dead in Ditch, Antietam, Maryland (Matthew Brady, photographer)

In a "ghost excavation", we focus on an ethnographic-specific past cultural production in a particular space (cf. Sabol 2013). In recent years, our research has concentrated on historic battlefields (location-specific) and the "culture of war" or "war cultures" (culture-specific), and the "culture of death" of mid-19th c. American Society. The experience of a battlefield production, from the perspective of the soldiers who fought there, and framed by a particular "culture of war", was pioneered by John Keegan in his book, *The Face of Battle* (1976). This is part of the field of Battlefield Archaeology, and today is part of what is now termed "Conflict Archaeology" (see John Carman, *Archaeologies of Conflict,* 2012).

An anthropological study of this archaeological record, which we focus on in a "ghost excavation", involves **"the multiple meanings and perceptions that individuals and groups at home and on the front lines, created in response to the conflict to endure its effects" (Wilson 2012).**

I propose that the paucity of any substantive data in most "ghost hunts" of "haunted" locations is a lack of a location-specific/culture-specific orientation in field work. I propose the problem is one of "ethnographic displacement". This is fieldwork that is **"more engaged in the analysis of space….than in actually experiencing social space as a sincere cultural participant" (Alexander 2006:53).**

Our fieldwork is a practice-led research that involves the production of data through participatory and immersive modes, rather than a strict adherence to a client/percipient interviewing model. We investigate what remains of a particular past production of space, the archaeological remains.

I propose that the existence of a "haunted" battlefield space, as opposed to a haunting sense of this place (perceived as monument battlefield construction, battlefield tours, and re-enacted events), is <u>not</u> separate from a space's varied past productions:

"Traces must be in some way related to social realities" (Ian Hodder, archaeologist, 1978).

As in archaeology, so in what remains of haunted space! There are no Roman centurions (or "demonic presences") that command a company of soldiers on an American Civil War battlefield, though the soldiers may have fought like "demons"! The history and documentation of "what" and "who" remains after the event of a battle must not be considered "paranormal". It must <u>remain</u> ethnographic, as part of the past production of human culture.

For many of us who investigate these battlefields, the fieldwork is all about "going home". It is not, however, <u>our</u> home. It is theirs. This makes these battlefields a potential landscape that should remind us of this (their) loss of family and cultural ties, 150 years after their physical fight has ended. Because of this loss of "home", a Civil War battlefield should <u>never</u> become a field of entertainment (or a "hunt" for presence).

The Civil War battlefield has been described in endless letters and memoirs that report these soldier's experiences on the battlefield:

"explosive death....mass dismemberment....splattered flesh; men without heads; men with both legs blown off at the thigh; disembowelings; catastrophic face wounds; brain matter showerings; living comrades blown into rags of bloody cloth and fragments of pale bone; or half gone but still able to talk or scream...." (Roper 2008:122).

How can "investigators", knowing this history (or not knowing it, or worse, ignoring it) still act like battlefields are places of entertainment, or a place to experience a "haunting" thrill?

These fields should not be explored as serene or peaceful landscapes. As Kent Gramm states:

"May they mourn, brood, scream, stare, cry, lament; may they growl and mutter; may they implore and regret, regret, regret!" (2002:35).

The Civil War battlefield is not an inactive place because some are still at war. These presences are not "at home". They remain on those fields of conflict. As an investigator of these Civil War battlefields, I must always ask myself this: is what he was, what he fought for, and what he believed, have anything at all to do with why I am here, and interested in "who" haunts this place?

It should! If not, it's merely entertainment. The phantom, that "shadow" of a person, that "orb" of a being, and that EVP of a lost and forgotten soul must be banished from our minds and vocabulary. A different image must replace them. The haunting myth must be exorcised, and the "ghost" made human again:

"Tenderly bury the fair, unknown dead,

Pausing to drop on his grave a tear".

Afford to these unknowns that remain, a trace of their humanness........

Photo 7: Fieldwork on the Battlefield

Investigators at Gettysburg, Pennsylvania

<u>Problems with the Archaeological Record</u>

Knowledge about the past, and its documentation, is a palimpsest, a series of chapters that remain as trace and vestige of particular past productions, even <u>contemporary</u> past productions. These historically (and habitually) produced spaces are continuously being modified through inscriptions of new knowledge, activity, and occupation. This creates new knowledge, images, and experiences, and erasures of older ones.

A haunted space, I propose, is a temporally-recurring palimpsest: an assemblage of sensory cultural elements that are manifesting in particular spaces. They are traces and fragments of what occurred (and what may be occurring) in that space (and what is occurring there today). These remains percolate over and over again from different times, events, acts, and cultural expressions or "signs" of past/current productions.

That is why an "excavation", I propose, is needed. It reduces the fieldwork to a controlled and systematic process of "unearthing" and documenting what remains of these past productions. These multiple layers of presence, a "surface stratigraphy" of remains, create a sensory bricolage that can "haunt" us if we do not control the process of manifestation during "excavation".

When one focuses on the socio-cultural production of space, one <u>must</u> understand that the concept ("production") applies not only to the object of study (what remains of past presence), it applies <u>equally</u> to the way our actions (as a contemporary presence) <u>also</u> create a production of space. We must be very careful in our fieldwork:

- To investigate is to potentially inscribe. We produce residual presence as a contemporary production.
- A non-contextual inscription (one that differs from what occurred in the past in a particular space) can create an erasure of some (or most) fragments of past productions!

An example of this is the "jogger" that was photographed during our "ghost excavations" at Burnside Bridge on the Antietam battlefield in Sharpsburg, Maryland (for a full description of this "excavation", please see Sabol 2012).

Photo 8: The "Jogger"

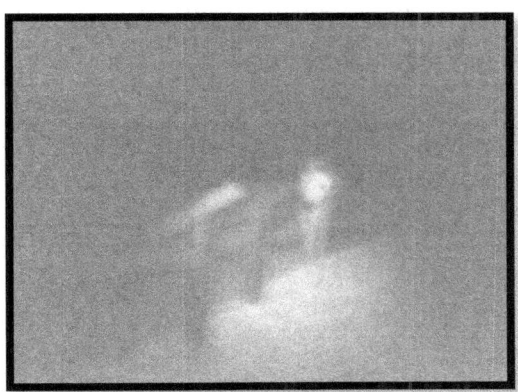

This "jogger", perhaps a contemporary, habitual act by a "live" person was <u>not</u> contextual to what occurred in that space in the past, which was the scene of intense and horrific combat on September 17, 1862 (part of the deadliest day of combat in American history). A "jogger" has suppressed (or "erased") what occurred there during the Civil War!

Those who "ghost hunt" these Civil War battlefields must be extremely cautious and accountable for what they do there! A "ghost hunter" here must always ask themselves this:

- Is what <u>he</u> (or she) was, what they fought for, and what they believed, have anything at all to do with why I am here? And why, am I interested in "who" may haunt this battlefield?

It should be more than mere contemporary entertainment! And it may erase what occurred there in the past! A contemporary "ghost hunting" presence on an American Civil War battlefield should <u>never</u> become demeaning, dishonorable, and unworthy to all those who fought there, those who died there, and those who may remain there!

Fieldwork on battlefields is not entertainment. What is a re-enactment but a sanitized contemporary version of an impression of a horrific history of deadly combat? Why are they permitted to "entertain" the living, when they don't have permission from those who remain?

We must become "witnesses" again to that event in history, and respect "what" and "who" may remain. The phantom, that "shadow" of a person, that "orb" of a being, and that EVP of a lost and forgotten soldier must be banished from our minds. A different image must replace it. The "haunting" myth must be replaced, and the "ghost" made human again:

"Tenderly bury the fair, unknown dead

Pausing to drop on his grave a tear".

We must ask ourselves (each time we investigate): what remains after our contemporary event/act?

- Is it a new inscription, or a past erasure (or both)?
- Is this new inscription part of the archaeological record of the past, or a production that has nothing to do with what occurred in that space in the past?

In our post-fieldwork analysis during a "ghost excavation", we discuss the production of space as an ontological condition, actively analyzing this production as an integral part of our own (and others) contemporary practices. We ask ourselves this:

- Are we re-covering the past; a contemporary-past "ghost hunt", or the habitual activity of a living individual?

A Battlefield Ethnography

"The military landscape provided us with a spatial order dedicated to sudden and violent movement, a set of relationships based on total subordination and anonymity, and a sensory experience based on death...."

- Jackson 1980:17.

Photo 9: The Civil War Battlefield

Union Attack, Marye's Heights, Fredericksburg, Virginia

This, however, is not the complete "ghost story" of why a Civil War battlefield becomes haunted. Any field analysis regarding a continuing Civil War presence on these battlefields must become an anthropology of war, a particular "culture of war", and the multiple meanings of "life" between individuals on the battlefield, and the family at home. It <u>must</u> include the responses, as particular options, that both made as an effect of large quantities of horrific battlefield encounters with the "end of life".

A battlefield is an ethnography of place, a culture of/at war. A "ghost excavation" is a record of my own efforts at understanding how this battlefield space was (and continues to be) occupied. It is the recovery of how particular sensory manifestations become a sound foundation for defining social continuance and communication in these battlefield spaces.

These are spaces that individuals, and large groups of men (that sometimes included women and boys) "inhabited", some for very brief moments in time, with intensity and high emotion.

The "excavation" of these battlefield spaces begins with an affected body (both literally and in the historical narrative), one affected with particular cultural beliefs about the "end of life", in a place where that "end" became a statistically-high possibility. The battlefield became a dwelling place, a "still point" in death for an improbable entity (a "ghost") in mid-19th c. society (before the outbreak of the Civil War) regarding this end of life.

This battlefield ethnography of haunted space does not <u>begin</u> with a "setting", a particular geographic space. It begins with an "end", in multiple physical spaces as the place of death, and the "end" of physical life. Setting, however, is important.

Setting sets the stage for why there are "ghosts" on these battlefields. This setting is "home", and the "household". These are familiar surroundings with family, and especially "Mother".

Setting becomes a domestic imagery of where these soldiers want to be located, and where they want to be when this "end of life" is encountered on the battlefield:

"(I) talk about home, let it be ever so homely, it would be a desirable change. I would be satisfied to lie on the bare floor....and my blanket to cover me and not say one complaining word...."

- **Thomas Reed, 21st Massachusetts (quoted in Murray 2001:167).**

The poet Walt Whitman, in his untiring efforts for caring for the battlefield wounded in military hospitals, frequently commented on the soldier's profound need for communications from home.

The songs of the Civil War also echo this sentiment for "home" and "mother", such as the following:

"Just before the battle, Mother

I am thinking most of you

While upon the field, we're watching

With the enemy in view".

- **Irwin Silber,** *Songs of the Civil War* **(1960:151-53).**

The distancing of death, as the "end of life", from the home and family created a need for a memory of the past (the proper "home rituals"), in an era becoming increasingly modern. The dead relied upon the living to remember them, and to continue to enact the proper rituals of mourning, of transition, and of transformation as a rite of passage from one form of life to another.

The "home" setting on the battlefield was replaced, many times, by "substitutes", the "band of brothers" one grew-up with, knew, enlisted together with, and with whom one fought alongside on these battlefields:

"It is awful to see the dead and wounded laying on the ground. If I am killed or wounded, my tent mates will write and let you know it, and send my money and pictures to you, for the boys are very nice fine boys and we think a great deal of one another".

- **Riley Norcott, 34th Illinois (quoted in Murray 2001:123).**

Substitutes also included, for those who were wounded and taken to field hospitals, those who cared for them there, and comforted them in their agonies during their "end of life". These would include nurses and local area residents, besides their fellow soldiers (even after they died):

"We went into the 'dead room'. There were several corpses there, each one marked with the name, company, and regiment of the deceased. Discarding the coarse coffins furnished by the government, we tenderly placed all that remained of our comrade in a neat coffin....and bore him (to) the foot of a tree bursting into bloom.... (where) we buried him...."

- **Henry Johns, 49th Massachusetts (quoted in Murray 2001:196).**

Louisa May Alcott, in her *Hospital Sketches,* stated that women, in the role of nurses, reminded the soldiers of **"mother and home"**. This was part of the 19th c. concept of domestic imagery, tied conveniently to the "good death", as a form of consoling the dying.

Though this was a supremely feminine task, it was used by both officers and one's fellow "band of brothers". These social codes on death and dying on the battlefield and in field hospitals provide a layered depth to the experience these soldiers felt. This layered depth must be fully explored in any analysis of "why" and "who" remain as "active" presences on these battlefields today.

The idea of:

"remembering home, dreaming of it....allowed men....to a certain extent, retain their pre-war identities" (Mitchell 1993:35).

It also allowed, I propose, these soldiers to retain their pre-war beliefs in the concept of the "good death". It was this "retention" in this belief system that led, propose, to the haunting of the battlefield by some of these soldiers.

The important cultural codes of experiencing the "end of life", amid the concepts of "home" and domestic imagery, and a "band of brothers" to help as "substitutes" with some of the "good death" rituals, shaped the options of these soldiers when that end came. It determined whether they experienced the "good death" or not. On those battlefields, as a place of death, dying the "good death", as the "end of life", determined whether one remained as a ghostly presence, or whether one went "home".

The idea of a "band of brothers" substituting for the family of a dying soldier was real, especially among Confederate soldiers, because:

"In nearly all regiments, officers and men knew each other before the war, attended school and church together, worked in the same fields, and courted the same young women. Independent-minded, these Americans accepted being led, not compelled, by friends" (Wert 1999:94).

<u>Photo 10: Did these soldiers die the "Good Death"?</u>

Dead soldiers in ditch, Gettysburg, Pennsylvania

These cultural codes, as integral components of the belief system of mid-19th c. American Society, governed and refashioned the geography of these battlefields. This is because "how" one died, with "whom", and with "what" rituals of the "good death" enacted there, determined the route of the dead through the battlefield: you remained or you "crossed-over".

Nineteenth Century American Society mourned well, long, and hard. There was an elaborate visual etiquette, behavior, ritual, and temporal parameters firmly in place. The ritual was socially-prescribed in countless narratives, texts, songs, and illustrations.

Dying was an <u>active</u> process, and not a passive one ("waiting"). This is an important part of the "culture of death": **"unattended death sparked terror and signified a great spiritual and emotional loss" (Saun 1980:98).**

Tom Zinser, an American hypnotherapist and soul release therapist, believes that it is the fear of death that is a key factor in distorting behavior and in depriving the dead of a "good death". In mid-19th c. America, I don't believe that this was the case.

A Civil War soldier, before a battle, did not fear dying on the battlefield so much as he feared not receiving or experiencing the rituals associated with a "good death". These rituals were an important part of the "culture of death". If the soldier did receive at least some ritualistic elements of the "good death", I believe he died in peace and "crossed-over".

Photo 11: What Happened to these Soldiers after Death?

A "ghost excavation" is a translation of this transition (or transformation) to a "haunted" battlefield. It imposes a framework and works within conventional spatial and temporal coordinates, but its context is not the present. It is the past.

Space, on the contemporary battlefield, becomes the "K.O.C.O.A.", a contextual militarily-defined space (for details, see Sabol 2009). Fieldwork moves from contemporary explorations to a participatory "excavation" back to the "culture of war" and Inherent Military Probability (I.M.P.), or how the soldier would have been trained to act, and what he would have experienced, in particular situations in these K.O.C.O.A. spaces.

As investigators, during a "ghost excavation", we become, during the performance practices, the "substitutes" for their families. We perform the rituals of the "good death" through acts that resonate with these past cultural codes.

The belief system of these soldiers, their ethnographic culture (the "culture of death") was inseparable from the reality of their deaths on the battlefield, as they performed the ritualistic practices of this military culture (the "culture of war") within the theatre of war.

The circumstances and character of their deaths, together with these engrained cultural codes (home, family, domestic imagery, band of brothers, the "good death") led, in some instances, I propose, to the haunting of these battlefields. The incompleteness of the ritual of the "good death" becomes an attachment so powerful, it causes a haunting.

There was a strong special ambiance to this attachment, located in specific K.O.C.O.A. spaces. Because of the powerful emotional synergy around, and in these spaces, there was an integration of the spatial (K.O.C.O.A.) and cultural ("culture of war"; "culture of death") environments.

Anthropologist Michael Taussig, in his book *Shamanism, Colonialism, and the Wild Man: A Study in Terror and Healing* (1991), states that **"the space of death is important in the creation of meaning and consciousness...." (1991:4).** Did the death of some of these soldiers create meaning (as a haunting attachment) and an "afterlife" consciousness in these spaces on the battlefield?

I propose that they did. War, and the tragic and horrific deaths on these battlefields, experienced far from "home" and family, constitute the immediate historical and socio-cultural background that produced these "ghostly" presences there.

There is more to a Civil War battlefield haunting than deadly outcomes. The horrific battlefield death, occurring in unprecedented numbers, is only part of this "ghost story". It is also the means by which they died, and what happened afterward, that becomes an important component of this "afterlife" story.

Avery F. Gordon, in her book *Ghostly Matters: Haunting and the Sociological Imagination (1998)*, has written:

"The ghost is not simply a dead or a missing person, but a social figure, and investigating it can lead to that dense site where history and subjectivity make social life. The ghost or the apparition is one form by which something lost....makes itself known....The way of the ghost is haunting, and haunting is a very particular way of knowing what has happened or is happening" (1998:8).

What is "missing", why some of these soldiers remain on the battlefield, is a "loss". It is the "loss" of the proper mourning rituals, anchored to the concepts of the "good death" and domestic imagery ("home").

Jeffrey A. Weinstock (2004) takes a similar stance:

"The ghost is that which interrupts the presentness of the present, and it's haunting indicates that, beneath the surface of received history, there lurks another narrative, an untold story that calls into question the veracity of the authorized version of events" (2004:5).

Those unknown, buried dead in mass graves had consequences, an untold story. It is to their families that the story remains untold. It is to us, today, that the "ghost story", the battlefield "ghost", emerges:

"Phantoms haunt; their appearances signal the potential emergence of a different story and a competing history" (Ibid: 6-7).

That different story is a real "ghostly" one. This is because **"phantoms participate in, reinforce, and exemplify various belief structures" (Weinstock 2004:8).** These belief structures are not contemporary ones (a "paranormal event"). They are historical-ethnographic ones.

This is a belief in the importance of the "good death". This is not a religious issue. It is a social one. The belief in a "good death" transcended religion. It was the belief of a society, not any one religion.

There is also the bio-politics (or lack of bio-politics) that is involved. During the American Civil War, because of necessity, and an undeveloped mortuary system (at least in the initial years of the war), there was little policy regarding the proper disposal of the dead. During this time, the dead became empty, meaningless, "bodies" of remains (rather than human beings). The dead were disposed of quickly, in mass (largely undocumented) grave sites, and without the proper cultural codes of the "good death". Some of these "unknowns" still haunt these battlefields!

Is an implication of this non-developed policy of properly disposing of the dead (in both a physical and cultural sense), in some of the deadliest battles (Shiloh, Antietam, Gettysburg, to name a few), the creation of an "afterlife" social existence for some of these neglected dead (fed also by their beliefs in a "good death")? Has this resulted in a recognition of presence today on these battlefields, perhaps even a **"co-belonging"** of the living and the dead?

If this theory is reality, it has enormous implications, induced by any society which, through forms of neglect, causes hauntings to occur in contemporary space (such as modern hospitals) as well as past space (the Civil War battlefield). Some other implications include:

- Questions of ethics – care and concern for the "afterlife" of past presence: the use of "ghost hunting" as "entertainment";
- Means of social interaction with the dead; and
- Relations between what is "life" and what are "forms of life", as a continuance of active presence from the past.

The Civil War represented the transformation of a society from one existing rhythm of movement and understanding of the world ("home"; the "good death"; ritual mourning) to another (the battlefield, far from "home"; horrific death without the proper rituals). The battlefield transformed the concept of death and the "end of life", and with it, an "afterlife" for some of these soldiers begins.

There is more substance to these "ghosts" and manifesting presence than mere metaphor for "something" that was lost or forgotten, or viewing these contemporary manifestations as a "paranormal" event. They may have a more literal existence.

I propose that many of these presences form part of personal biographies from the experiences of these men in combat:

"Personal biographies are formed through encounters with particular places in the cultural landscape and the recognition and understanding of the panoply of codes constituting their meaning" (Tilley 1993:82).

These codes are the <u>cultural</u> codes that are associated with the "culture of war" and the "culture of death" that were part of the life and death experiences of these soldiers on these battlefields.

What happens when these "ghosts" break out of their usual confinement as perceived (or ignored) presences by contemporary science, and begin to really "haunt" us with their manifestations? Is it a taunt to scare us, or is it really a cry for assistance, a need to be accorded the rites (their right) of a "good death?

"Ghosts are the unwelcome carriers of an occulted history; they show us how we screen, and thus protect ourselves, from the past. They function, to be sure, as agents for the reconstruction of historical memory....ghost stories might be effective....as a means by which repressed histories can be brought back to the surface" (Huggan 2008:168).

This concept of a repressed history, manifesting in the present, does have a contemporary ethnographic basis that goes beyond the use of the "ghost" as a metaphor.

Contemporary Ethnographic Research

The "ghost", as an interactive social presence, has been analyzed in relation to the socio-cultural manifesting context in which it arose. In the case of the American Civil War battlefield "ghost", the context is both social (the "culture of death") and historical (the Civil War "culture of war").

Contemporary ethnographic work has shown the importance of ghostly presence as a consequence of recent, traumatic history. A recent ethnographic study of emigrants to the United States, *Consoling Ghosts: Stories of Medicine and Mourning from Southeast Asians in Exile* by Jean M. Langford (2013), concerned the intervention of ghosts in their lives. This study is:

"not so much an ethnography of particular communities – as a mediation of forms of engagement with death and the dead that are....marginalized....and on the power of ghosts...."

This "haunting" was based on the institutionalized exclusion or neglect of the bodies of the dying and dead, those who died in violence, whose bodily remains were lost, or whose funeral rites were incomplete. These dead did not die a "good death", similar to those soldiers on American battlefields during the Civil War.

This is an example of contemporary fieldwork that is not so much relative to cultural differences based on "spirit beliefs" as it is the discovery and analysis of histories through which "ghosts" and "spirits" have critical (and interactive) contemporary roles. Other examples of this contemporary research include Mueggler (2001), and Kwon (2008).

In *Ghosts of War in Vietnam,* Heonik Kwon (2008) examines the **"Vietnamese experience and memory of the Vietnam War through the lens of popular imaginings about the wandering souls of the war dead".** People have become haunted by soldiers who died far from home and family ties, and who received improper burial rites. These "ghosts" were brought about by the changing nature of the Vietnam battlefield, the mobility of civilians and combatants alike.

This mobility cut across traditional family-based commemorative practices, and involved human remains that were unrelated to kinship ties. The author explores **"the intimate ritual ties with these unsettled entities....as well as the actions of those who hope to liberate these hidden but vital historical presences from their uprooted social existence".** These actions, however, are treated as **"fantastical"**.

Do they, however, have roots in history, and in a reality that haunts other places of violence and horrific consequences? Is the situation in the study area (formerly South Vietnam), where bodies were "improperly" buried (becoming the "unknown" dead), similar to the mass burial trenches of unknown dead on American Civil War battlefields? Is the lack of familiar ties, and a "good death", in both cases, a preface to real haunting phenomenon?

Are these "ghosts" of the displaced dead ("foreign" to a locale; far from "home"), and as "unknowns" in mass graves, create a "place attachment" to the spaces where they died? Did this lead to haunted spaces today at these sites? Are these dead waiting for "kin" to bring them home?

In contrast to the "metaphorical" haunting of the "ghosts" of Vietnam, the "consoling" ghosts of the Southeast Asian emigrants are perceived as real presences. The dead, those victims of war and violence, return, as one example, because their funeral rites were incomplete, similar to the "loss" of the proper rituals of the "good death" of some of the battlefield dead of the American Civil War.

The "end of life" in both cultures (both "cultures of war") denied the social importance of the dying (or the unavailability to complete the proper social rituals), an important component of the "culture of death" in these societies (contemporary Southeast Asian; mid-19th c. America).

There are ways for the living to face death, proper rituals to follow, and means to conduct relations with the dying. In both cases, there was a displacement: there was no relation between the "culture of war" and the "culture of death". The result, in both cases, I propose, was a contemporary haunting by interactive "ghosts"!

In *The Age of Wild Ghosts: Memory, Violence, and Place in Southwest China,* Erik Mueggler (2001) discusses life in this part of China as an era **"inflected by eruptions into the present of unreconciled fragments of the past** (characterized by a century of violence)**, often personified as the ghosts of people (or spirits) who had met bad ends...."**

The book chronicles a story about **"what it means to live as a community in the aftermath of violence",** a resonance (although temporally- more limited) to the period of the American Civil War, in the aftermath of so much violence and death. In one (China), the "ghost" is a metaphoric consequence (?); in the other (mid-19th c. America), it is more than a metaphor of what occurred on those horrific battlefields.

In Southwest China, it was the "death" of a dream of a lost community that fueled these manifestations, reinforced by stories of hunger and injustice, killings and suicides. In 19th c. America, it was the "death" of an individualized "good death", amid the ruins of countless battlefields. In both cases, these "deaths" created "ghosts". Questions, however, remain: are both histories metaphorical, or is the presence of these "ghosts" real (in one, or the other, or both)?

One thing is certain. Like its counterpart in pre-Civil War America, in Southwest China the "house" (home) is important as a foundation for social relations. The "home", its occupancy, the rituals enacted within, all prevented the manifestation of "ghosts" after death.

The violence, and horrific nature of a battlefield, or the violence caused by outside influences in China, created, I propose, a different "death". It was a death that was not familiar or domestic-based. It opened a means for "ghosts" to appear.

<u>The Social Technology of Death</u>

Social technologies determined how to die the "good death", and how to perform the proper rituals of mourning. Social technology is defined as knowledge about how to **"do something" (Hacking 1996:80).** That doing something was to die the "good death"!

The social technology of dying, as the "end of life", the "good death", consisted of the following material cultural expressions:

- Particular actions with material objects as "triggers" that composed the process of the "good death". This included location (a bed in the "home"), visual presence ("Family"), and mourning attire ("Black"), to name a few;
- Performance as memory: the family did certain acts, said certain words, and continued mourning for a specified period, depending upon the age and sex of the family member; and
- Reading (the Bible), writing (the "wishes"), and speaking (the "acceptance") the ritualistic "formula".

The "good death" created a "time to die" during an explicit performed situation. It meant an **"objective time" (Gell 1992),** facing the obvious, "death". The ritual, by converting the dying process into a socially-performed time (cf. Flaherty 2011), governed at least some province of time.

These social technologies controlled an important human temporality: the time before death, as the "end of life" (not its continuance). The "good death" was an important social process of dying in a particular time and space.

The rituals of the "good death" controlled, however superficially and momentarily, the unpredictability of the timing of actual death. These rituals became a form of acceptance: a willingness to let go and die (not an intentionality to remain). It is the appearance and use of these social technologies that allowed the family to gain some sense of the inevitable, and the ability of said family members (and the dying individual) to accept the inevitable.

Photo 12: The "Good Death"

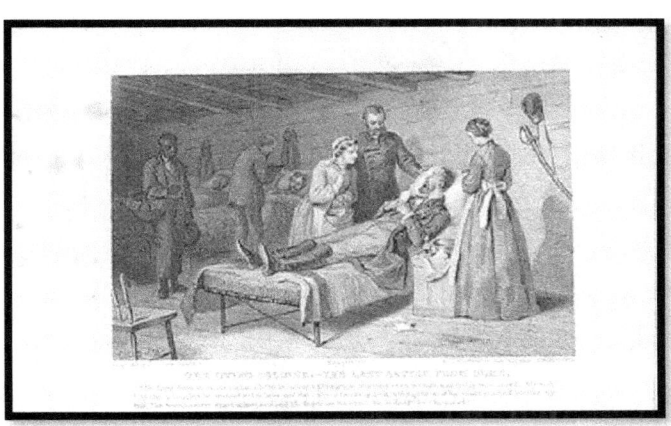

Illustration: "The Dying Soldier – The Last Letter from Home"

These social and psychologically-familiar controls were "lost" (in many cases) on the battlefield. On a Civil War battlefield, the governance of time did not occur. The Civil War battlefield compromised the "good death" process, but did not <u>always</u> eradicate the ritual. There were "substitutes".

This sociable process, with its defined social technology, created a **"technology of memory" (Thomas 1993)** which became critically "lost" for some of these soldiers on these Civil War battlefields. It was the loss of this "technology of memory", I propose, that became more important to "who" remains than the actual physicality of a battlefield death, no matter how horrific it was. It led, I propose, to socio-cultural battlefield hauntings.

To understand these particular types of battlefield hauntings, one must give meaning to the <u>cultural</u> codes behind ghostly presence on these battlefields. A battlefield haunting is <u>not </u>inevitable because of particular kinds (horrific injuries), degrees ("numbers"), and characteristics (age) of battlefield death, but rather the lack of ritual timing during the last moments before death occurred. The interval before (the "good death"), the temporality of death (the "ritual" process), became "lost", so "life" continues.

One of the means to communicate with these soldiers, during a "ghost excavation", is to act out those "unperformed" rituals of the "good death". This is resonance, not measurement. This is performance, not mere observation (and waiting for something to happen). This is doing these acts, not asking questions ("Is anyone here?"), or asking them to perform ("Can you make the lights blink?"). We, not they, perform.

It is this consciousness associated with (and deprived of) the "good death" that is the distinguishing "sign" of what it means to die and remain human (as a "ghost" of a former culture) on these battlefields. The non-performance of the "good death" rituals, at the end of one's time, shapes the possibility of the existence of an "afterlife consciousness" of some of these soldiers who fought on these battlefields.

In death, without the social technology in place (or at least some of the ritual replaced by "substitutes" for family and a "home" environment), a social relationship (albeit obligation) continues, instead of being annulled at death.

Identity and social technology remain. To determine if, and "who", remains, the investigator must retain (through resonance) an "identity" and obligation to those social codes associated with the "culture of war" and the "culture of death". That is why any form or semblance to entertainment on these battlefields is grossly inhumane and immoral! Through the "good death", an individual, spiritual liberation is achieved. Without it, a haunting is a distinct possibility.

In the ritual of the "good death", the living (a soldier's family) become intertwined with the dying in a shared social reality. During a "ghost excavation" on these battlefields, we ourselves become immersed with the dead, as we share with them, through our performance practices, that past social reality.

Besides sharing, however, we must also serve as those "surrogates" for family, and perform some of those rituals of the "good death". This is a particular notion of dying and death, as a transforming and haunting interactive process. It is a continuation of sociality (though in an altered form), forming an integral part of continuing social presence on these battlefields. (for examples of our use, in a "ghost excavation", of these rituals of the "good death", please see below).

Photo 13: Performing the Ritual of the "Good Death" on a Civil War Battlefield (Antietam).

Investigators during a Ghost Excavation, Antietam National Battlefield, Sharpsburg, Maryland

Photo 14: Performing the Ritual of the "Good Death" (Gettysburg Battlefield).

Investigators during a Ghost Excavation, Gettysburg National Battlefield, Pennsylvania

Home and the Household

"Most everyone thinks of the cheerful faces and blazing fires of home with a strong desire to be there".

- E.A. Brown, Captain 6th Wisconsin, November 24, 1861 (Brown Letters, State Historical Society of Wisconsin).

"I tell you it makes a person think of home and their dear parents and wish to be there".

- John Gibbon, Wisconsin corporal, October 5, 1862 (after the battle of Antietam) (Gibbon Papers, Historical Society of Pennsylvania).

The household is the basic unit of social organization. Anthropologists identify three components of households:

1. Co-residence;
2. Domestic functions; and
3. Familiar relationships.

In mid-19th c. America, all three components served to define the "setting" where a "good death" was realized. It was individuals who lived within the household who performed the ritual of the "good death". The ritual of the "good death" was a function of domestic imagery, home and familiar surroundings. It was the family who surrounded the individual at the "end of life".

The mid-19th c. household, prior to the outbreak of war in 1861, is the key concept in understanding both the "culture of war" and the "culture of death" as it transformed during the Civil War. The Civil War and the battlefield death changed forever the structure of American households, their social interactions, their rituals, and how they viewed the "end of life".

A direct result of this social and cultural transformation had two lasting effects:

- For the living, it led to the spread of Spiritualism and the concept of "domestic séances"; and
- For some of the dead, it resulted in continuance, the haunting of particular locations outside the household, particularly the Civil War battlefield.

The presence of a "ghost soldier" on a Civil War battlefield is a specter whose appearance is out of time (what haunts these battlefields from the period of the Civil War). This haunting is not only the manifestation of a "ghost", but also what those "ghosts" represent: a familiar household member who is out of place.

It is time to recover that household member, and bring that someone "home". This is not the work of a "ghost whisperer", or a spirit release practitioner. This is cultural work, part of military reality of the "culture of war" of the American Civil War. It has a long history. The idea of returning the dead to be buried at home has been a part of U.S. policy since the mid-19th c.

The "ghost" of the Civil War battlefield is out of place, appearing somewhere else than "home". This displacement of time and space is the <u>direct</u> result of the loss of ritual acts associated with the "good death" in a place called "home", and at a time nearing the "end of life". Thus, "what" and "who" are out of context is "someone" in space, a space in time, and outside that culture (and those ritual acts) of mid-19th c. America.

The "home" a traditional female domain, becomes haunted by the absence (not presence) of particular male bodies. The battlefield, a traditional male domain, becomes haunted by the absence of "home", "family" and "mother", the traditional presences associated with the "good death". The female, normally located in the "home", now wanders these battlefields, as a forceful haunting presence, in search of lost family loved ones.

Mothers and wives:

"came to take personal charge....Timid Victorian women who had never before left their own village found themselves far from home....determined to get their men home" (Ernst 1999:175).

This female movement from the "home" to the battlefield was both common and widespread:

"Desperate families both North and South traveled by the hundreds to battlefields to search in person for missing kin" (Faust 2008:127).

The Civil War battlefield "ghost" that haunts the contemporary landscape is profoundly historical and cultural whose meaning (out of space –not the home) and function (to go "home") is not the same as other types of American hauntings, such as the "home bodies" or the **"Stay-Behinds"** described by Hans Holzer:

"Stay-Behinds is a term I have invented. It refers to earthbound spirits or ghosts who owe their continued residency in what may have been their long-term home to the fact that they don't want to leave familiar surroundings" (Holzer 1997:631).

The Civil War battlefield "ghost", deprived of the "good death" at "home", wanders on these battlefields, sensing this loss of place and cultural ritual. His appearance was not preventative. A particular way of dying in battle that was common (not unique), complicated by the existence of the battlefield "unknown" and the mass, inhumane burial trenches, resulted in these haunted landscapes today:

One has to know....to know is to know who and where, to know whose body it really is and what place it occupies....One has to know who is buried where...." (Derrida 1999:9).

These battlefield "ghosts" appear because they are displaced from home, and the familiar ritual of the "good death", which should have ended their life here on earth. It didn't. They remain (at least some of them) because they are not buried in the traditional "ritualistic" way of the time period (before the advent of national, state, and local cemeteries). There is no "family plot" on these battlefields.

This is a model of a haunting, and a spectral scenario, that raises the dead of the past into the present in very special ways. These ways are associated with the "culture of war" and the "culture of death" of that period in American history. It wasn't the end of life. It was just its future....for now.

It's time to help some of these soldiers to finally "go home". What follows in the next section of the "ghost story" is a brief summary of our "ghost excavations" on the Antietam battlefield. This section details our efforts to bring "home" several of these soldiers who may remain on this battlefield (for a more detailed account of these "ghost excavations", please see my books: Sabol 2012; Sabol 2013).

Photo 15: "Ghost Excavations" at Burnside Bridge on the Antietam Battlefield in Maryland.

Battlefield "Ghost Excavations"

Photo 16: Burnside Bridge Today

A "ghost excavation" is never about going in search of an "orb", a "shadow", a drop in temperature, or "ghost box" static. It is a rescue mission, an attempt to recover "someone" from the past who was a cultural being, had a social history, and who is still manifesting a form of cultural life and behavior.

A social system (the "culture of death") disappeared on the Civil War battlefield, with believers and practitioners (the soldiers) not being able to complete (in many instances) the rites of a "good death".

The ritual of the "good death" could not sustain itself, as a cultural continuity of this "culture of war", during the demanding social conditions (spanning four horrific years) that were associated with the massive loss of life during the American Civil War. Its functionality failed (a "ritual failure"), due in part to the mass burials of "unknown" soldiers, and the obliteration of recognizable bodies of men as a consequence of destructive fire power.

The result was a change on these battlefields to the concept of the "end of life". This "ritual failure" had wide social, economic, and political implications. The social system transformed and, in the process, left only traces or "signs" of the consequences of that transformation, the "battlefield ghost".

Robert Blauner, in the journal *Psychiatry* (1966), demonstrated (using anthropological literature) that the early death of important members of the family resulted in ghost traditions. Did this tradition, a ghostly presence, transform the cultural tradition of the "good death" into the manifestation of battlefield "ghosts" after the Civil War?

We came to the Antietam battlefield, the site of the bloodiest day of combat in American History, to find out. The manifestations that occur there today, we hypothesized, must be something indexical (as a "sign") of intentional agency that reflect remnant patterns of the "culture of war" and the "culture of death" of the period of the American Civil War.

These intentional manifestations must also become present in the <u>absence</u> of any perceivable "agent", especially if the manifesting action is repeatable in a contextual situation. This rules out the possibility of random spontaneous phenomena or confirmation bias. And it adds credibility when a particular context is used.

The haunting that continues today at Burnside Bridge, Antietam Battlefield, Maryland is, I propose, a semiotic system (traces of cultural "signs"). On this part of the battlefield, there are distinct physical and acoustical territories of the "culture of war" and the "culture of death". These "territories" of haunted space encompass and define a "live" Civil War battlefield.

Our research and fieldwork there, meant to "unearth" and map this semiotic system, aimed at recovering the architectural features ("geopsychic architexture"), a **"technology of memory" (Thomas 1993),** of "what" and "who" remains from the engagement that was fought there on September 17, 1862.

<u>Photo 17: The Battle for Burnside Bridge</u>

The Union Perspective

This fieldwork was a non-evasive, and minimal intrusive, "excavation" performance of the original "K.O.C.O.A." spaces, as they were defined in 1862. The contemporary setting of Burnside Bridge is a synecdoche stage of the theater of war of the American Civil War: it is now limited to traces and fragments of that "culture of war" and "culture of death" of 1862.

Our "ghost excavations" there are meant to resonate with the existing "technology of memory" (as a system of ritualized practices and acts of war and about death and dying). Our "excavating" performances were centered in particular "K.O.C.O.A." spaces, and were associated with particular situations, behaviors, and experiences that were enacted (and sensed) there, including Inherent Military Probability (or I.M.P.).

Our understanding of "who" remains rests on two basic archaeological principles:

- **"Traces must be in some way related to social realities" (Ian Hodder, 1978)**; and
- **"To what extent do changes in materializing presence preserve the traces of previous organizations"? (Gavin Lucas, archaeologist).**

We wanted to know if the manifestations we recorded were related to the "culture of war" and the "culture of death" of the time period in question (Civil War). We also wanted to know if these manifestations deviated from behaviors, acts, or vocal expressions that were associated with these two cultural expressions of mid-19th American Society. Were these "signs" of presence that we were recording, the "signs" of presence of an American Civil War soldier in combat at Burnside Bridge?

No sign of presence ("haunting" or otherwise) has meaning in and of itself. A test for meaning must be performed during the "excavation" process: our use of contextual scenarios of "ritualized" behaviors, related to these two "cultures", must be recognized, and acted upon, by a particular "targeted" social community (such as those companies of soldiers who fought on both sides of Antietam creek).

"Ritual activities frequently involve a practical remembering effected through the experience and manifestation of symbolic material items" (Barth 1987:75).

Photo 18: Burnside Bridge (September 1862).

In order to test a remembrance of the "culture of death", especially the importance of "home", we had one of our investigators, Mary Becker, read a letter from a Dr. George Bronson, 11th Connecticut, a surgeon who survived the battle. In the letter, written to his wife, he describes the engagement at Burnside Bridge.

Also, in the letter he describes a **"great loss"**:

"Some villain rifled my pockets....and what I valued most my needle book containing the little lock of hair you put in. No money would have bought it. It was not the value that I cared for, but the giver."

The letter, and particularly the lock of his wife's hair, served as a **"symbolic material item"** for the concept of domestic imagery (a remembrance of "home"). While Mary was reading this part, we recorded a male voice begin to sing, and in the lyrics was the distinct word "home". You can hear this recording at www.ghostexcavation.com.

Philosopher Charles Peirce has said:

"An idea is only clear if it produces the effect of recognition among a company of interpreters" (1878).

Did the "idea" of reading the letter produce a significant meaning (the importance of "home" = "domestic imagery") for a company (or a single individual) of remaining soldiers of the 11th Connecticut? Was social meaning established in and through the ritual of reading that letter, which became the **"symbolic material item"** for the "ghosts" (or a "ghost") of the 11th Connecticut? We will continue to test this hypothesis in future "excavations" at Burnside Bridge.

Photo 19: Dr. George Bronson

Photo 20: Dr. Bronson's wife

Mary Anne Bronson (nee, Lewis)

Another example of why "ghost soldiers" may continue to haunt this battlefield lies in the differences in the disposition of the Union dead and the Confederate dead here. The bodies of Union soldiers were interred (and re-interred) first. Many of the Confederate dead, killed in a non-Southern state, were left for days on the field of battle.

Many were interred in mass graves of "unknowns". Others were hastily buried, and remain missing, even today. One who is still "MIA" is Lt. Colonel William Holmes, 2nd Georgia. One of our objectives during "ghost excavations" at Burnside Bridge was to locate the burial place of Holmes.

In the "search" for Holmes, we followed what was recorded in historical narratives:

"Desperate families, both North and South, traveled by the hundreds to battlefields to search in person for missing kin" (Faust 2008:127).

In the 1860 census, two women were listed in the Holmes household in Georgia. We had two female investigators, dressed in period clothing, portray these women. They searched along the stone wall, adjacent to the bridge and Antietam creek, with lanterns, calling out his name, hoping to locate his presence (if he still remains there) and bring him "home" to Georgia.

Photo 21: The Search for Colonel Holmes

Photo 22: The Search for Colonel Holmes

In their search, "someone" answered" (multiple times). A male voice, responding to these women's pleas, told us where he is "buried". This same voice is repeated, with the same location given, on two subsequent "ghost excavations" there. You can hear these recordings at www.ghostexcavation.com.

Did "Lt. Colonel Holmes" respond? We will continue the search in 2014, this time aided by ground-penetrating radar which will allow us to locate any disturbances in the area where a voice said "he" was buried.

These are just two examples (at Antietam), linking the "culture of war" and the "culture of death" to contemporary manifestations on that battlefield. More data on these "ghost excavations" can be found in two other books (see Sabol 2012; 2013).

In the future, we will continue to test this relationship between the manifestations of "ghost soldiers", and a relationship between their perceived presences and the "cultures" of war and death on other Civil War battlefields. The results of these "ghost excavations" will be published in subsequent books, and a summary of this fieldwork will also subsequently be found on our website at www.ghostexcavation.com.

Summary

The results of war have frequently been cited for their association with political and economic change. The American Civil War, besides these changes, also caused a social change in the concepts of death, dying, and the afterlife. American Society was called upon to take an active responsibility at "the end of life", and, because of the war, was forced to come to terms, sometimes directly, with what occurred <u>after</u> death.

This book attempted to show how cultural behavior, shaped by particular (not peculiar) attitudes and cultural beliefs about death, facilitated acts and actions both on the battlefield and <u>also</u> on what happened, in some cases, <u>after</u> the death of the combatant.

In an 1862 sermon, Stephen Elliott, an Episcopal bishop, stated the following:

"Men and women approach death in ways shaped by history, by culture, by conditions that vary over time and across space. Even though we all have our dead, and even though we all die, we do so differently from generation to generation, and from place to place".

We all die. But we all don't die the "good death". History has recorded, for the past three thousand years, that some do remain after death. Some of these "ghosts" are metaphors, serving as lessons to be learned, or to instruct us about social or personal issues. However, not **all** "ghosts" are metaphors, or popular "images" which teach us about "life".

"Ghosts" are imagined and perceived in the likeness and character of one's own times. The American Civil War "ghost" is no exception. Some contemporary versions of that "ghost" go beyond the simple formula of a metaphor to a "ghostly" manifestation of a "spirited" presence. This "phantom" is based on a "popular culture" belief system, guided by technology. It is not based on <u>their</u> culture, those who lived and died during the American Civil War.

This is a book about <u>that</u> culture, specifically the "culture of war" of the American Civil War, and how that culture relates to the "culture of death", the "good death". It concerns a different "ghost". It is about the **"ars moriendi" (the "art of dying").** This was a domestic, peaceful, "homely" passing in the presence of family.

Civil War families sought knowledge that their loved ones lived long enough to embrace God, surrounded by some semblance of a "good death". Loved ones yearned for final words or messages that communicated this sentiment.

All of these battlefield deaths affected the home life in ways that viewed death, their now dead (or missing) loved ones, and how they approached and carried out their grieving. It is how the relationship between two cultural traditions and ritual performances (the "culture of war" and the "culture of death") led to a haunted battlefield.

This is <u>not</u> a "paranormal" realm, as many who "hunt" these "ghosts" today believe. It is a cultural world. There are no physical laws that predict a haunting. There are cultural rules and roles. There is no standard "ghost hunting" methodology, governed by electronics. There is cultural production, social belief, and semiotic "signs" of presence that we must interpret.

The Civil War battlefield "ghost story" is not about the impact and meaning, manifesting today, of the war's (or a particular battle's) death toll in sheer numbers and horrific carnage. It is about the battlefield's impact on, and violation of, a society's prevailing cultural assumptions about the "end of life".

It <u>is</u> about a "good death": "when" and "where" that occurs, under "what" circumstances, to "whom", and "why" did it occur. These five potential points of a "haunting" continue today, as does the concept of the "good death".

Contemporary principles of a "good death" (Smith 2006) include:

- **"to know when death is coming, and to understand what can be expected"**;
- **"to be able to retain control of what happens"**;
- **"To be afforded dignity and privacy"**;
- **"To have choice and control over where death occurs"; and**

- "To have time to say goodbye". (2006:129-130).

The only principle that is missing, from the Civil War era, is to be buried at home in the family plot.

The period of the Civil War, called by some a **"medical Middle Ages"**, did exhibit a partial re-construction of the "familiar" ambiance of the "good death", rather than an ability to systematically prevent its occurrence, or prolong life.

In the important role of "playing" family members, many medical staff took the death bed scenario seriously and personally. They substituted their medical role for a familiar one, all too often ignored by hospital staff today.

Photo 23: A Civil War Hospital

Washington, DC

In this process of re-orientation and expansion of medical care, by providing emotional assistance to the dying, the medical corps during the Civil War eventually re-defined the end of life, the beginning of a new "life" and, I propose, the prevention of a haunting. Are contemporary hospitals more haunted than Civil War hospitals because of this different medical role, aimed at the "good death", which has become largely lost today?

The Civil War, and one of its cultural expressions, the battlefield, represented a dramatic shift in incidence (frequency), experience (sudden) and location (far from "home") of the "end of life". Ordinarily, death <u>was</u> buried in battle, but so was, for many, the ritual of a "good death".

This harvest of "bad" death produced the possibility of multiple haunting fields, especially among the Confederate rank and file, where **"nearly every household mourns some loved one lost"**. Loss was commonplace, but the "good death" was not. It produced the "ghost".

Death was no longer experienced individually in the home, where approximately 85% of pre-war death occurred there. On the battlefield, it occurred in groups, amid a "band of brothers".

The actuality of this widely-shared experience, without proper ritual reinforcement, produced a battlefield haunting. As one Confederate soldier observed, death **"reigned with universal sway"**. It ruled not only over the battlefield, but home life and the search for those who remained missing from family and home. It demanded attention and response then. It continues to do so today.

This contemporary attention and response is not, in any of its characteristics, a form of entertainment. It must be based on the principles and beliefs of those cultures of mid-19th c. America from which these hauntings sprang, and remain, embedded on these battlefields.

In the relation between the cultural codes (the "culture of war" and the "culture of death"), an investigation on these battlefields must attend to three aspects:

1. The process of death and dying;
2. The event of a battlefield death; and
3. The status of being "dead".

Photo 24: A Civil War Battlefield Investigation

Investigators James Castle and John Sabol at the 11th Connecticut

These battlefield "ghosts" are about humans, those Americans who lived that experience that went beyond "seeing the elephant"! This experience was savage and brutal. It was an encounter with the presence of death, and what that encounter produced, in some cases, on the contemporary battlefield.

Death on those battlefields did not simply happen. It required specific acts and agents, a process of dying. It required participation. It produced a landscape. It was experienced. In that experience, a "ghost" was born.

That "ghostly" presence was not a given! It is work to die. It is work to haunt. It is intentional and purposeful because it is based on belief, and circumstances. It becomes situational: how, and under what circumstances, die death occur?

It is also work for us to deal with the dead in this way. It requires respect, not demand. It requires empathy, not provocation. It is about them, not us. It is about loss, and a ritual that remains incomplete.

It is <u>still</u> about "home" and family. Some of these soldiers remain because their "end of life" is still an open book. It remains a "ghost story". They haunt. We must write the "end" to that story, make it a "homecoming", by completing the ritual, and not entertaining ourselves in the process.

This is not a type of fieldwork to remove them (but to move them on). Sometimes, though, this does involve physical remains even when the visual (surface) evidence is absent. An excavation can do that. What lies beneath our field of inquiry may be the physical remains of someone still lost from a battle that occurred 150 years ago.

What has become lost in Civil War histories is how the war affected the <u>future</u> occupation of these battlefields: how the war's deadly consequences led to altered conceptions of how life should end, how it did end for many, and the consequences of that transformation. The work of this deadly conflict continues today. No one should entertain the notion that it is simply just about the "ghosts".

These battlefields are not a game of numbers: how many died there. A "ghost excavation" is meant to change that statistical attitude through a change in latitude, one that is vertical, not one measured on a horizontal plane. By "digging-deep" into the past of history, and "deeper" into a location's haunted nature, we can recover a future where the "ghosts" become human again.

From the viewpoint of the (a) "good death", not all battlefield fatalities were equal. Because of this, many Civil War battlefield spaces go beyond the vision and perception of serene, well-manicured landscapes <u>of</u> memory. They become soundscapes <u>in</u> memory, the memory of the "culture of war" and the "culture of death".

Hopefully, these thoughts may encourage us today to take more responsibility for our field actions, our understanding of Civil War death, and of those "bodies" of memories. These soldiers will remain until the moment when their "ghost bones" are returned from whence they came, the family "home".

Photo 25: The Family of a Civil War Soldier

General Rufus Ingalls Family

<u>Photo 26: A Family "Waiting" at Home</u>

Appendix

"Ending Vocal Performance" ("E.V.P.")

"They say, the tongues of dying men

Enforce attention, like deep harmony

Where words are scarce, they are seldom spent in vein"

- **John of Gaunt (Richard II, William Shakespeare).**

The "last words" are an important part of the "ritual" of dying. Prior to the Civil War, they were usually performed (85% of the time) at "home". On a battlefield, quite often, this didn't happen, even when a "brother" (or comrade-in arm) substituted for a real "family".

Why don't battlefield "E.V.P." record an "E.V.P."? Is it because most "ghost hunts" are not culturally-attuned to the soldier's cultural codes of the "culture of war" and the "culture of death"?

Think about it. Why are there no recordings of the "final words" of a dying soldier? Why are there no cries for "Mother" on the battlefield? Why are there no pleas, from dying men to go "home"? Has any "ghost hunter" performed as a family member in a "hunt" for their presence? How many "ghost hunters" have enacted the ritual of the "good death" on a "haunted" battlefield? Think about it....

Closure: The Beginning of a New "End"

The absence of identifiable bodies, even as subsequent archaeological remains, creates uncertainty. It leads to the birth of a haunting for the living. Related to the concept of the "good death" was closure. Families went to great lengths, especially the female members, to bring the men "home".

These females, many of them previously restricted to the domestic scene, extended a familiar reach out to those battlefields in search of loved ones. Mothers and wives

"came to take personal charge of a wounded man's care....Many insisted on arranging transport for their loved ones, sure they would mend best at home....Timid Victorian women who had never before left their own village found themselves far from home....determined to get their men home" (Ernst 1999:175).

Eventually, this had consequences because of the large economic burden involved, besides the social and emotional trauma. What if the family member still remained lost?

It led, as one consequence, to the spread of Spiritualism which "brought" the boys "home" without spatial movement (on the part of the women). Families were allowed, Spiritualists proposed, to personally hear those original "E.V.P." A Spiritualist newspaper, the *Banner of Light,* proposed to seek out dead soldiers, and find out if they died the "good death". Family members, at this stage, were not hoping for a "live" lost loved one, but rather for a "dead" one, now at peace, who had experienced the "good death".

Faust (2008), in her book *The Republic of Suffering,* shows how a whole industry rose in an attempt to preserve this notion of a "good death". This included the development of "home séances". In the 1860's, a planchette (a pre-Ouija board) became a popular item in the home.

But there is a problem with the rise of and use of Spiritualism in this scenario of hauntings related to the loss of the rituals of the "good death". One explanation for the rise of Spiritualism is that there was a

"need for consolation following bereavement, especially in the wake of the American Civil War. Spiritualism soothed those who had suffered loss by assuring them that the dead were not really gone...." (Weinstock 2010:411).

These dead **"continued to dwell in a nearby invisible realm, invited communication with the living, and awaited a happy future meeting with those who had mourned them in this life" (Castle 1995:133).**

The problem is that this is a focus on the living, not the dead. It was based on consoling the living, not performing the rituals for the dead. It did draw attention to the possible reasons why the dead were willing to communicate or, more importantly, that they "haunt". It re-focused attention on the "home", rather than the battlefield, where the haunting phenomenon originated.

I am currently researching this relationship between the Civil War home, haunted battlefields, and the spread of Spiritualism and Spiritualist beliefs in these homes, and the possible consequences relative to the continuance of these battlefield hauntings.

Bibliography

Alexander, Bryant 2006. *Telling Twisted Tales: Owning Place, Owning Culture in Ethnographic Research* in *Opening Acts: Performance In/As Communication and Cultural Studies.* Judith Hamera, Editor. Thousand Oaks, California: Sage. pp. 49-74.

Bal, Mieke 2010. *Exhibition Practices.* PMLA 125, No. 1.

Barth, F. 1987. *Cosmologies in the Making: A Generative Approach to Cultural Variation in Inner New Guinea.* Cambridge: Cambridge University Press.

Bergson, Henri (1908) 1988. *Matter and Memory.* New York: Zone Books.

Blanco, Maria del Pilar and Esther Peeren 2013. *The Spectralities Reader: Ghosts and Haunting in Contemporary Cultural Theory.* London: Bloomsbury.

Blauner, Robert 1966. *Death and Social Structure* in *Psychiatry* 29:378-94.

Braude, Stephen 2003. *Immortal Remains: The Evidence for Life After Death.* London: Rowman and Littlefield.

Broad, C.D. 1962. *Lectures on Psychical Research.* London: Routledge.

Bubandt, Nils 2012. *A Psychology of Ghosts: The Regime of the Self and the Reinvention of Spirits in Indonesia and Beyond. Anthropological Forum: A Journal of Social Anthropology and Comparative Sociology.* Volume 22, Issue 1: 1-23.

Carman, John 1999. *Bloody Meadows: The Places of Battle* in S. Tarlow and S. West (ed.) *The Familiar Past? : Archaeology of Later Historical Britian.* London: Routledge.

2012. *Archaeologies of Conflict.* London: Bloomsbury.

Castle, John H. 1995. *Letters Received.* RG 92 A-1, 397-A National Archives and Records Administration, Washington, D.C.

Delaplace, G. 2013. *What the Invisible Looks Like: Ghosts, Perceptual Faith, and Mongolian Regimes of Communication* in *The Social Life of Spirits.* Edited by Ruy Blanes and Diana Espirito Santo. Chicago: University of Chicago Press.

Derrida, Jacques 1999. *Rights of Inspection.* (Translation: David Wills). New York: Monacelli.

Detzer, David 2004. *Donnybrook: The Battle of Bull Run, 1861.* New York: Harcourt, Inc.

Ernst, Kathleen A. 1999. *Too Afraid to Cry: Maryland Civilians in the Antietam Campaign.* Mechanicsburg, Pa: Stackpole Books.

Espenshadet, T., Robert L. Jolley, and James Blegg 200s. *The Value and Treatment of Civil War Sites* in *North American Archaeology.* Vol. 23, No. 1: 39-67.

Faust, Drew Gilpen 2008. *This Republic of Suffering: Death and the American Civil War.* New York: Alfred A. Knopf.

Flaherty, Michael G. *The Textures of Time: Agency and Temporal Experience.* Philadelphia: Temple University Press.

Gell, Alfred 1992. *The Anthropology of Time: Cultural Constructs of Temporal Maps and Imagery.* Oxford: Berg.

Glassie, Henry 1977. *Archaeology and Folklore: Common Anxieties, Common Hopes* in *Historical Archaeology and the Implication of Material Things.* Leland Ferguson (Ed.). Special Pub. 2. Columbia: Society for Historical Archaeology. pp. 23-35.

Gordon, Avery F. 1998. *Ghostly Matters: Haunting and the Sociological Imagination.* Minneapolis: University of Minnesota Press.

Gramm, Kent 2002. *Somebody's Darling: Essays on the Civil War.* Bloomington: Indiana University Press.

Hacking, Ian 1996. *Rewriting the Soul: Multiple Personality and the Sciences of Memory.* Princeton: Princeton University Press.

Hawkes, Jacquetta 1951. *Guide to the Prehistoric and Roman Monuments of England and Wales.* Cardinal Books.

Holzer, Hans 1997. *Ghosts: True Encounters with the World Beyond.* New York: Black Dog Eleventhal Pub. Inc.

Huggan, G. 2008. *Interdisciplinary Measures: Literature and the Future of Post-Colonial Studies.* Liverpool, U.K: Liverpool University Press.

Jackson, J.B. 1980. *The Necessity for Ruins.* Amherst: University of Mass. Press.

Keegan, John 1976. *The Face of Battle.* New York: Penguin Books.

Kwon, Heonik 2008. *Ghosts of War in Vietnam.* Cambridge: Cambridge University Press.

Langford, Jean M. 2013. *Consoling Ghosts: Stories of Medicine and Mourning from Southeast Asia.* Minneapolis: University of Minnesota Press.

Maher, M. and George P. Hanson 1995. *Quantitative Investigation of a "Haunted Castle" in New Jersey* in *Journey of the American Society for Psychical Research.* 89:19-50.

Mitchell, Reid 1993. *The Vacant Chair: The Northern Soldier Leaves Home.* New York: Oxford University Press.

Mueggler, Erik 2001. *The Age of Wild Ghosts: Memory, Violence, and Place in Southwest China.* Berkeley: University of California Press.

Murray, Stuart 2001. *A Time of War: A Northern Chronicle of the Civil War.* Lee, Mass: Berkshire House Publishers.

Oakeshott, Michael 1933. *Experience and its Modes.* Cambridge: University of Cambridge Press.

Orr, David G. 1994. *The Archaeology of Trauma: An Introduction to the Historical Archaeology of the American Civil War* in *Look to the Earth: Historical Archaeology and the American Civil War.* Edited by Charles R. Geier Jr. and Susan E. Winter. Knoxville: University of Tennessee Press. pp. 21-35.

Quinton, A. 1975. *The Soul* in *Personal Identity.* J. Perry (Editor). Berkeley: University of California Press. pp. 53-72.

Relph, E. 1981. *Rational Landscapes and Humanistic Geographies.* New York: Barnes & Noble.

Roper, Robert 2008. *Now the Drum of War: Walt Whitman and his Brothers in the Civil War.* New York: Walter & Co.

Sabol, John G. 2009. *Battlefield Hauntscape.* Bloomington, Indiana: AuthorHouse.

2012. *Burnside Bridge: Expanding the Contemporary Reality of Past Interactive Interactions.* Brunswick, Md: Ghost Excavation Books, Inc.

2013. *Digging Up Ghosts: Unearthing Past Presences at a Haunted Location.* Brunswick, Md: Ghost Excavation Books, Inc.

2013. *The Production of Haunted Space.* Bedford, Pa: Ghost Excavation Books, Inc.

Saum, Lewis O. 1980. *The Popular Mood of Pre-Civil War America.* Westport, Conn.

Shanks, Michael 2012. *The Archaeological Imagination.* Walnut Creek, Ca: Left Coast Press.

Sheldrake, Rupert 2012. *The Science Delusion: Freeing the Spirit of Enquiry.* London: Hodder & Stoughton, Ltd.

Silber, Irwin 1960. *Songs of the Civil War.* New York: Columbia University Press.

Smith, R. 2006. *A Good Death* BMJ 320: 129-130. 8 November.

Taussig, Michael 1991. *Shamanism, Colonialism, and the Wildman: A Study in Terror and Healing.* Chicago: University of Chicago Press.

Thomas, Julian 1993. *The Politics of Vision and the Archaeologies of Landscape* in *Landscape: Politics and Perspectives.* Barbara Bender (Ed.). Oxford, U.K: Berg. pp. 19-48.

Tilley, Christopher 1993. *Art, Archaeology, Landscape (Neolithic Sweden)* in *Landscape: Politics and Perspectives.* Barbara Bender (Ed.). Oxford, U.K: Berg. pp. 49-84.

Watson, Richard A. 1991. *What the New Archaeology Has Accomplished* in *Current Anthropology.* Volume 32, No. 3 (June) pp. 275-91.

Weinstock, Jeffrey 2004. *Introduction: The Spectral Turn* in *Spectral America: Phantoms and the National Imagination.*

Edited by Jeffrey Andrew Weinstock. Madison: University of Wisconsin Press. pp. 3-17.

2010. *The American Ghost Story* in *A Companion to the American Short Story.* Edited by Alfred Bendixen and James Nagel. pp. 408-423.

Wert, Jeffrey 1999. *A Brotherhood of Valor.* New York: Simon and Shuster.

Wilson, Ross J. 2012. *Landscapes of the Western Front: Materiality During the Great War.* London: Routledge.

Wooffit, Robin 2010. *Toward a Sociological Parapsychology* in *Anomalous Experience: Essays from Parapsychology, and Psychological Perspectives.* Edited by Matthew D. Smith. Jefferson, North Carolina: McFarland and Co., Inc. pp. 72-91.

Biographical Note

Photo 27: The author

John Sabol holding a shadowbox of bullets found
near Burnside Bridge, Sharpsburg, Maryland

John Sabol is an archaeologist, cultural anthropologist, actor, and author.   As an archaeologist, he has documented and recorded the manifestations of past soundscapes at haunted ruins. As an actor, he has appeared in more than 35 movies, TV series, and educational TV programming, including the Sci-Fi classic, **Dune (1984)**, and the A&E TV series, **Paranormal State.** He has written 22 books on his fieldwork, methodology, and his personal experiences on location filming, and his work at haunted ruins around the world. He has been a frequent guest on numerous radio and internet talk shows, among them, <u>Beyond the Edge Radio</u>, <u>The Paranormal View</u>, <u>Para X Radio</u>, <u>Blog Talk Radio</u>, <u>The Grand Dark Conspiracy</u>, <u>ParaNation</u>, and Rusty O'Nhiall's "Mysterious and Unexpained" on PsiFM (Australia). He has also worked on international educational documentaries (in Spain).

He is the director of several documentaries that are accounts of immersions into past ethnographic soundscapes at historic sites now in ruin. In these ruins, he has recorded manifestations of past cultural behavioral fields, including the "culture of war" on several Civil War battlefields and, most recently, coal-mining cultural vestiges and traces of past presence at Centralia, Pennsylvania. He has organized (and playec a role in) theatrical "stagings" and "ghostings" (site-specific performances) at haunted locations which recorded "spiritscapes" at these haunted locations.

He has developed numerous scripts and storyboards for these documentaries, as part of a "ghost excavation" series of mediated venues. He has presented video clips and audio tracks of these documentaries at various scientific conferences and popular culture expositions in Europe, Canada, and the USA.

Recent speaking appearances include, but not limited to, *Popular Cultural Conferences in Washington, D.C. and in Niagara Falls, Ontario, Canada;* the *G.H.O.S.T.S. Conference in Ontario, Canada;* several conferences in England including with the *Royal Geographic Society* (Britain's premiere exploration Society), *Seriously Strange Conference in Bath, England;* at the *University of Kent, Canterbury;* CHAT *(Contemporary and Historical* **Archaeology** *in Theory), University of York, York, England, and TAG (*Theoretical **Archaeology** Group), at the *University of Berkley, California* and at the *University of Buffalo,* respectively.

He can be reached via email at cuicospirit@hotmail.com. His IMDb site is: **http://www.imdb.com/name/nm1254777/** . The website is: **www.ghostexcavation.com**. He can be found on Facebook ("Ghost Excavations with John Sabol", "John Sabol, The Ghost Excavator", and "Beyond the Paranormal").